Anne Broyles

Priscilla and the Hollyhocks

Illustrated by Anna Alter

Charlesbridge

In memory of Edna May Broyles and Dottie Stewart—A. B.

For Trina, and all she does to help children overcome their circumstances.
A special thank you to Kay Bullock, who grows Priscilla's hollyhocks and
kindly gifted me with a box of seeds.—A. A.

Text copyright © 2008 by Anne Broyles
Illustrations copyright © 2008 by Anna Alter
All rights reserved, including the right of reproduction in whole or in part in any form.
Charlesbridge and colophon are registered trademarks of Charlesbridge Publishing, Inc.

Published by Charlesbridge
85 Main Street
Watertown, MA 02472
(617) 926-0329
www.charlesbridge.com

Library of Congress Cataloging-in-Publication Data
Broyles, Anne, 1953–
    Priscilla and the hollyhocks / Anne Broyles ; illustrated by Anna Alter.
        p. cm.
    Summary: A young African American girl is sold away from her mother as a slave,
and then later is sold to a Cherokee Indian, but eventually she is bought by a
white man who not only sets her free, but adopts her into his family of fifteen children.
Based on a true story; includes instructions for making a hollyhock doll.
    ISBN 978-1-57091-675-5 (reinforced for library use)
[1. Slavery—Fiction. 2. Hollyhock—Fiction. 3. Trail of Tears,
1838—Fiction. 4. United States—History—1815–1861—Fiction.]
I. Alter, Anna, 1974– ill. II. Title.
PZ7.B82447Pr 2008
[E]—dc22   2007002281

Printed in China
(hc) 10 9 8 7 6 5 4 3 2 1

Illustrations done in acrylic on Strathmore Bristol board
Display type set in Fiddlestix, designed by Ronna Penner for Typadelic;
    text type set in Goudy
Color separations by Chroma Graphics, Singapore
Printed and bound by Regent Publishing Services
Production supervision by Brian G. Walker
Designed by Susan Mallory Sherman

When I was young and still wore slavery's yoke,
I was saved by hollyhocks, and a white man's kindness.

Freedom filled my dreams, but I was born a slave's child.

"She'll fetch a pretty penny," Master said as he loaded Ma up in a wagon like a steer led to slaughter. Ma turned her anguished face to me, raised one hand in farewell.

I lacked strength to wave back, tho' I 'spect my eyes mirrored her sorrow.

I pined after Ma.

Old Sylvia recollected me 'twas Ma planted hollyhocks along the white picket fence by the cow pond.

"Your ma made hollyhock dolls like this, Priscilla," Old Sylvia said. She took the beauteous pink flower in her gnarled brown hands, pushed and pulled it into shape, set it sail on the cow pond. I watched my flower dolly float and felt my mother's smile.

Six years I played like any child. The cow pond was my home, the cows my family. I could turn a hollyhock blossom into a pretty lady in no time flat. Then I was put to the work for which Master said I had been born.

"Work hard and keep still," Old Sylvia told me. She put a dust rag in my hands.

My first days in the Big House, I felt the weight of Master's rules. I played invisible, silent as the walls, and hoped no one would pay me no mind. I learnt not to jump when Master hollered, but my insides was a'quiverin'. Late at night, as I lay alone on a quilt in the attic, I 'membered the sound of other slaves' screams as Master beat them.

My poundin' heart echoed the blows Master struck against black bodies.

Sundays I fled to the hollyhocks. I watched my dollies float, dance 'cross the pond.

My smile escaped at the joy of it.

One mornin' when I served Master his porridge, his hand stung my cheek.

"Tarnation, you're slow, gal!" He jumped up, knocked over the chair, stormed out with a slammed-door curse. I clutched the unspilled bowl in my warm, tremblin' hands, took it back to the kitchen.

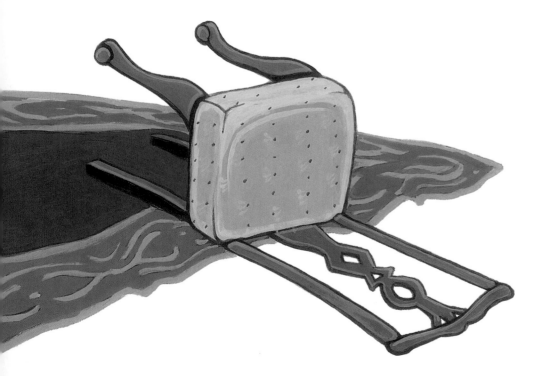

"Might as well eat," Cook said, and added a dollop of sugar to the porridge.

I grinned, picked up a spoon.

Visitors streamed in and out of the plantation. To them I weren't no diff'rent than wallpaper. Then came a man who whistled a cheerful tune as he strolled around the property. His name was Massa Basil Silkwood.

He asked me questions. I answered, hands quiet on my apron as I'd been taught. Weren't often anyone wanted to hear about Ma.

"You're a bright little thing," he said. "You should go to school." I thought my ears'd gone crazy.

"What happens at school?" I asked.

"Students learn reading, writing, and arithmetic."

"I want to learn it all," I said, even though I'd never heard of 'rithmetic.

Massa Silkwood gave a friendly laugh, then became serious.

"I don't hold with slavery," he said sadly. "A child like you deserves more."

I stood taller and watched him as he walked away.

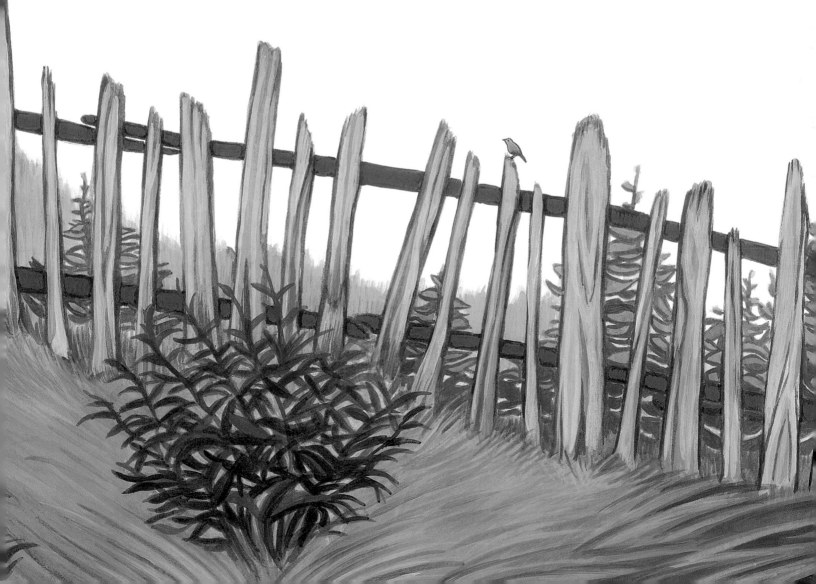

Master died soon after.

"Things a-gonna change," Old Sylvia warned.

I snuck to the cow pond on a Tuesday when the light was fadin' from the sky. I gathered seeds from the tall, spindly plants, stuffed them into my apron pocket.

Within weeks I stood on the auction block. Could the white men sizin' me up see how small and scared I felt? Never mind what price they set for me; I knew I wasn't the same as Master's cows, horses, furniture. A red-skinned man in a turban paid my price, took me away. I ne'er saw Old Sylvia or Cook again.

BOOTS, SHOES, HATS, & CAPS.

J&P.

AUCTION & NEGRO SALES.

OFFICE

2520

Another plantation, same life.

I learnt my duties in the Cherokee's house. I did my work and kept still.

The Indian and his wife didn't holler, but still they owned me.

I emptied chamber pots, dusted furniture, said "Yessir," "Yessam," even to little children. I was ten years old.

I scattered hollyhock seeds, made myself a Sunday hiding place: home.

My hollyhocks sent up tall, green stems, flowered the second spring. Wasn't much I wanted to 'member from my first home but Ma. Pink hollyhocks kept her livin'. Surely if I thought on her, she might think on me, too, where'er she was.

Time passed. White folks wanted more land, made a law to push Indians out of their homes. I didn't need Old Sylvia to tell me that change was a'comin'. Again I hid hollyhock seeds in my pocket. My Cherokee master's family and I was rounded up like animals with thousands of other Indians. Soldiers locked us behind tall walls where we suffered the long, hot summer. I fingered the seeds in my pocket and held back my tears.

Come autumn, the soldiers moved us. As far as I could see, a line strung out of horses, buggies, wagons, sad folk marching. All of us forced toward a place we didn't know.

We walked and walked. Snow fell. Roads froze. Soldiers' bayonets prodded us forward. We climbed mountains, forded rivers, trudged along our weary way. Sometimes I didn't think I could put one foot in front of t'other. We walked across states and through the months.

My Cherokee master's oldest son died from fever, was buried in shallow, cold ground on the side of the road. My mistress's hollow eyes told her sorrow; she wanted her boy back.

One cold December day, our parade passed through a town. Despite the stingin' wind, my eyes lifted to gaze on stores, homes, townsfolk lookin' at us.

I stared.

On a hotel porch stood a man I knew.

"Massa Silkwood?"

He knew me, asked my story, listened as the words spilled from my cold mouth.

"Think there'll be a school for me where they're takin' us?" I needed the promise of learnin' to help me walk those weary miles.

I saw his thoughts tumblin' in his head.

"Bless you, child," he said at last. His face was sad.

I could scarcely pull myself away, but I didn't want my master to come lookin' for me. I turned, left the white man on the porch.

The memory of Massa Silkwood's kind eyes warmed me some. That night, as we camped on the frosty ground, a buggy pulled up. My Cherokee master scowled to see Massa Silkwood. The two men stood together, glanced at me, spoke low. Massa Silkwood handed the Cherokee a bag of gold that held my freedom.

"Come, Priscilla," Massa Silkwood said.

I ne'er looked back.

Massa Silkwood set me free, but t'weren't the end of it.
Home we went to a family who claimed me slave no longer,
daughter once more. Fifteen brothers and sisters were given me;
in a trice, I had father, mother, family. My heart still ached when
I thought of Ma, but she would've wished me happy.
Again I shook hollyhock seeds from my pocket.

Grow, I sang to the seeds.
Bloom, I commanded the plants.
Safe, I told myself.
Home.